blues journey

by Walter Dean Myers

illustrated by Christopher Myers

holiday house/new york

For Joyce,
W. D. M.

To Karen and Dean,
C. M.

Jacket illustration adapted from a photograph by Eudora Welty
with the permission of Russell & Volkening as agents for the author.
Copyright © 1989 by Eudora Welty

Text copyright © 2003 by Walter Dean Myers
Illustrations copyright © 2003 by Christopher Myers
All Rights Reserved

This artwork was created with blue ink, white paint,
and brown paper bags.

The text type is Garamond 3 Bold.

Printed in the United States of America
www.holidayhouse.com

Library of Congress Cataloging-in-Publication Data
Myers, Walter Dean, 1937–
blues journey / by Walter Dean Myers; illustrated by Christopher Myers.
p. cm.
ISBN 0-8234-1613-5 (hardcover)
1. Blues (Music)—Poetry. 2. African Americans—Poetry. I. Title.
PS3563.Y48 B58 2003
811'.54—dc21   2001016645

ISBN-13: 978-0-8234-1613-4 (hardcover)
ISBN-13: 978-0-8234-2079-7 (paperback)

ISBN-10: 0-8234-1613-5 (hardcover)
ISBN-10: 0-8234-2079-5 (paperback)

Blues, blues, blues,
blues, what you mean to me?
Blues, blues, blues,
blues, what you mean to me?
Are you my pain and misery,
or my sweet, sweet company?

Going on a journey,
looking for my supposed-to-be
Going on a journey,
looking for my supposed-to-be
I'm riding that blues highway,
and Lord, it's riding me

Hollered to my woman,
she was across the way
Said I hollered to my woman,
she was across the way
I said I loved her truly, she said,
"It got to be that way"

Heard the top deck groaning, yes, and the ocean roar
Heard the top deck groaning, yes, and the ocean roar
Heard my brother crying till I couldn't hear no more

O Lord, O Lord,
Ain't it hard when your brother's crying
And you don't hear him anymore?

Blackbirds fly, hound dogs howl and bark
Yes, blackbirds fly, you know hound dogs howl and bark
I see my true love sitting, crying in the dark

Blues, won't you free me,
let all this suffering cease?
Said blues, won't you free me,
let all this suffering cease?
Give me a feather pillow,
and let me rest in peace

Pain will push and poke you,
despair will scrape the bone
Pain will push and poke you,
despair will scrape the bone
Misery loves company,
blues can live alone

The root woman told me
that my day was coming soon
The root woman told me
that my day was coming soon
Soon's a mule reads the Bible,
and Christmas comes in June.

The preacher climbs the mountain,
but the devil gets his dues
You know the preacher climbs the mountain,
but the devil gets his dues
A poor man gets his kicks,
fast dancing to the blues

I know you don't want me, you cast my love out to the sea
I said I know you don't want me, there goes my love out to the sea
I'm fishing for affection, hope your heart comes in to me

I'm busting sod on Parchman's,
if the sun don't lay me low
You know I'm busting sod on Parchman's,
if the sun don't lay me low
There's nine kinds of dying
a rich man will never know

Life can be so hard,
living in a two-room shack
You know how hard it is, child,
living in a two-room shack
Ain't nothing in your parlor,
a little less in back

Strange fruit hanging, high in a big oak tree
Strange fruit hanging, high in a big oak tree
You can see what it did to Willie,
can you see what it does to me?

The thrill is gone, but love's still got my heart
The thrill is gone, baby, but love's still got my heart
I can feel you in this music, and it's tearing me apart

I gave my woman money, I offered her my hand
Gave her *all* my money, said, "Baby, take my hand"
She smiled from here to Sunday, then spent it on another man!

(Now you know that's wrong!)

I was standing at the crossroads, didn't know which way to go
Standing at the crossroads, didn't know which way to go
My heart was pulling one way, my head said take it slow

The road is long, the moon is hanging low
The road is long, blood moon is hanging low
Past time to rise, past time to cut and go

                    Skipped out of Memphis, 'cause I was on the news
                    Skipped out of Memphis, 'cause I was on the news
                    Rode to Chicago in a freight car with the blues

My landlord's cold, cold as a death row shave
My landlord's so cold, cold as a death row shave
Charged fifty cents for a washtub, three dollars for my grave

If you see a dollar, tell it my full name
If you see a dollar, honey, tell it my full name
Say I'm being sociable, and it can do the same

I'm half scared of dying, half scared of being strong
I'm half scared of dying, half scared of being strong
Guess that's why I end up staying in that raging storm too long

Blues, blues, blues,
blues, what you mean to me?
Blues, blues, blues,
blues, what you mean to me?
Are you my pain and misery,
or my sweet, sweet company?

Blues, blues, blues,
sliding through the night
Blues, blues, blues,
sliding through the night
If you looking for a soft bed,
I'll leave on the light

Time Line

1865	With the end of slavery, rural black musicians begin playing wherever they can find an audience.
1902	Gertrude "Ma" Rainey and the Rabbit Foot Minstrels perform "The Blues" in their traveling show.
1912	William Christopher "WC" Handy publishes "The Memphis Blues."
1912	Bessie Smith sings with the Moses Stokes troupe.
1914	"WC" Handy writes "The St. Louis Blues."
1914	Blind Lemon Jefferson plays throughout the South. His fairly relaxed, almost swinging style, with complex guitar accomplishment, is known as the Texas Sound. The Texas Sound was a contrast to the hard-driving Delta Blues.
1920	Mamie Smith records "Crazy Blues," the first recording of the blues.
1923	Bessie Smith records "Down Hearted Blues."
1929	Charley Patton records the "Mississippi Bo Weevil Blues." The Delta Blues, of which Patton might be the best example, are more uptempo and incredibly raw. The lyrics reflect the hard lives, desperate loves, and often violent deaths of blacks in the Mississippi Delta.
1930	Huddie "Leadbelly" Ledbetter is sent to prison at Angola, Louisiana, for attempted murder. He will later record blues, prison songs, and work songs.
1936–37	Robert Johnson does a series of recordings, including "Me and the Devil Blues."
1939	Billie Holiday's rendition of "Strange Fruit" becomes both a popular song and a stirring protest.
1941	McKinley Morganfield, known in show business as "Muddy Waters," makes his first records for Alan Lomax. Much of what we know about American folk music, including blues, folk songs, and gospel, is the result of the collections and recordings made by Lomax.
1947	Sam "Lightnin'" Hopkins records "Can't Get That Woman Off My Mind" in Houston, Texas.
1951	Chester Arthur Burnett, known to the blues world as "Howlin' Wolf," records "Moanin' at Midnight." He and Muddy Waters lead a switch from acoustic guitars to electric guitars and establish the Chicago Sound as a distinctive blues variation.
1960	B. B. King, already popular among blacks in Memphis, is discovered by white musicians and, along with his guitar "Lucille," becomes a national figure, expanding the scope of the urban blues.
1960s	Many white blues players emerge, such as John Mayall, Eric Clapton, Paul Butterfield, and Bonnie Raitt.

Blues Glossary

BLACKBIRDS FLY: Blackbirds were often used as a symbol for African Americans. Blackbirds "flying" or dreaming about flying became a symbol for escaping misery.

BLUES: A distinctive kind of music, most often associated with the African-American experience but now recognized as an American art form combining African and European musical forms; the state of being low in spirit.

CROSSROADS: A frequently used phrase in blues lyrics. The crossroads is a place where an important decision is to be made, often the decision to do right or wrong.

THE DEVIL: Often depicted as tempting good people to do the wrong thing.

FAST DANCING: While much of the blues involved slow music, faster versions were used for dancing.

FEATHER PILLOW: For a poor man, having a pillow was a luxury; having a feather pillow was even better.

FREIGHT CAR: Illegally hopping onto a passing freight train was a cheap, if dangerous, way to travel.

HOLLERED: Early blues can trace much of its origin to a blend of African music traditions and English lyrics. Early blues consisted of the kinds of call and response phrases found in African music. The American version of these were called "hollers."

HOUND DOG: Hounds were used to chase slaves, and later prisoners. It was used in this sense in blues jargon, and also for a man "chasing" a woman.

JOURNEY: Few blues players were men with a lot of money. Traveling, whether to find a better job or a better life, is a common theme.

MEMPHIS: The early blues originated in rural areas of Georgia, the Carolinas, and the Mississippi Delta. As the players moved out of these areas, they took their blues with them to cities such as Atlanta, Memphis, and Houston, and later to Kansas City, Chicago, and Detroit.

PARCHMAN'S: A very harsh prison in Mississippi. Many blues songs deal with prisons, chain gangs, and the rough life of men living on the edge.

SOFT BED: A soft bed was often the best thing a poor man could hope for.

STORM: Much of the language of gospel music and the blues is in a kind of code. The singer does not want to say aloud what he really means. Being in the storm means being in hard times such as slavery, poverty, or segregation.

STRANGE FRUIT: It was a woman, Billie Holiday, who popularized this haunting song that refers to lynching.

THE THRILL IS GONE: As the blues developed in the cities and before broader audiences, the lyrics became less raw. But the themes remain the same. The well-known blues player B. B. King had a hit with a song with this title about a love affair that has gone cold.